THE
DEPRESSION
BOOK

ISBN 0-9614754-3-9

Meditation Center
P.O. Box 91
Mountain View, CA 94042
(415) 966-1057

Zen Monastery and
Interfaith Retreat Center
P.O. Box 1994
Murphys, CA 95247

- printed on recycled paper -

Introduction

We are offering this little book neither as an explanation of nor as a cure for depression. Please do not conclude that we are saying you shouldn't seek treatment or counseling. The primary point of this book is to suggest that depression, like anything else in life, can be received as a gift that will aid you in your spiritual growth. If you are willing to find compassion for yourself in the midst of the dull pain of depression, you will, perhaps, see how this is so.

As with the Center's other titles, this book is only loosely organized and tends to repeat itself—not unlike life. Also, like our other books, it is handwritten in an effort to slow the reader down so that awareness can touch the heart as well as the head.

In loving kindness,
Cheri

Foreword

An essential part of seeing clearly is finding the willingness to look closely and to go beyond our own ideas. There are many things in this book that go against what most of us have been conditioned to believe and think. When you read something that seems wrong or doesn't make sense, see if you can just slide it onto a back burner, remaining open to whatever truth there is in it. You might see it differently after you have been considering it for a while.

It is good to keep in mind that if the answers you already have were working for you, you wouldn't still be looking. It takes a lot of courage to step into uncharted territory. We're not going to say this journey won't be scary, but we can promise it will be worthwhile.

So you're depressed...

This book suggests that this is your best
opportunity to see
how you cause yourself to suffer,
to accept that process,
to embrace yourself,
and to let go in compassion
                    and end the suffering.

RIGHT NOW!
not later, when you're feeling better.

THREE STEPS
you could take while depressed

1. Pick up this book.

2. Accept the pain and be as kind to yourself as possible.

3. Appreciate yourself for having the willingness to do 1. and 2.

FOR CONSIDERATION:

The state of
DEPRESSION
is not the problem.

The process of
DEPRESSING
is the problem.

If you are depressed, ask yourself,
"What am I depressing?"

When depressed —

You don't want to <u>deny</u>
                    the experience
              nor
do you want to <u>indulge</u> it.

A friend comes to you and says,
   "My husband just left me."
You don't say,
   "good riddance. He was a toad,"
                 AND
you don't say,
   "Here, take these pills. Suicide is best."

SO WHAT DO YOU DO?

☞

4.

EACH TIME YOU ARE DEPRESSED,
stop and turn
your attention inward.

Imagine that you are someone you have no
reason to dislike. Pay attention to all your
feelings and begin to write them down.
No analysis, just allow it to come out like
a volcano. Spew it out. Express it in
whatever way. Stay with yourself (this
person you like) until you express everything you need to express. Go through
all the feelings that arise until it seems
like you get to the end of it.

If writing things down is hard for you,
try talking into a tape recorder, painting,
drawing, or sculpting.

The point?
When you do this kind of process,
you will begin to see patterns.

5.

You will begin to see the steps you take that lead to self-rejection and depression. You will notice your fears and assumptions and conditioned reactions to circumstances. It will begin to become clear that depression is something YOU DO, not some larger-than-life ogre to which you are victim.

YOU CAN DO THIS
FOR YOURSELF.

What we're moving toward is letting go of everything that keeps us from
BEING PRESENT WITH OURSELVES.

And the first and last thing
we'll encounter is
fear.

We're afraid of how we feel,
afraid of who we are.

6.

The importance of understanding
depression in general
and yours specifically:

Your depression is not random.

You feel,
   think,
   say,
   and believe the same things
                        every time.

Perhaps <u>what</u> you are depressing changes.
<u>How</u> you depress remains the same.

The only way we can know what is going on
is to sit down with an open mind
and pay attention.
If we watch
closely enough,
we notice that there are sensations in our
bodies that go with depression.

They don't vary.
They're the same every time.

We have a labeling system that goes with
those sensations. In this case, the label
is depression.

With this label comes a learned response,
the self-talk — everything we've been
taught to believe about depression.
What it is
What it means
What I am for feeling it
What will happen as a result
How the future will be

8.

When that talk starts, we have an
emotional reaction to it.
　　　I don't want this.
　　　I am afraid.
　　　This is too painful.
　　　Oh no, not this again.

And then comes a conditioned behavior
pattern which is usually avoidance/escape.
　　　I should quit my job.
　　　I've got to leave town.
　　　I need a drink (or drug).
　　　I want a divorce.
　　　I'm going to kill myself.
　　　I can't function. (paralysis)

SEQUENCE:　　　sensation
　　　　　　　　thought
　　　　　　　　emotion
　　　　　　　　behavior pattern

THESE ARE GOING ON ALL THE TIME,
　　　not just in depression.

If we are willing
to pay close enough attention,
we notice that in depression:

the sensations in our bodies
                    don't vary,

the thoughts in our heads
                    don't vary,

the emotional reactions
                    don't vary,

the impulses toward certain behaviors
                    don't vary,

and this chain of events
DOES NOT VARY.

(ED.'S NOTE: THIS IS a BIG CLUE.)

As children,
we learned that when we operated
from who we are, we got into trouble.
We learned
         that there is something
                        wrong with us.

We don't want to have that experience
again so we try harder and harder to
be the person we're supposed to be.
What we are suggesting is
THERE NEVER WAS
                ANYTHING
                        WRONG WITH YOU.

It's okay to be who you are,
okay to have all your feelings.
That's what sentient beings have —
                        feelings.

II.

We believe that if we don't get our hopes up, we won't be disappointed.

"If I'm always disappointed, disappointment won't be so disappointing."

"If I'm not too happy and optimistic, I won't have so far to fall when the bad times hit."

The place where most people can recognize that is the times when they've been feeling good for a while and then they start getting nervous that it won't last. This is commonly known as "waiting for the other shoe to drop."

BELIEF:

If I maintain a low grade depression, maybe I can shield myself from real unhappiness.

(ED.'s NOTE: If this page describes you, have you ever asked yourself if this process ACTUALLY WORKS?)

Being depressed is like wearing sunglasses with black lenses. When you have them on, everything looks dark.

What color lenses would you assign to other life experiences such as
joy, fear, love, and sadness?

When we respond to circumstances of our lives by putting on the dark glasses of depression and despair, we are responding from lifetimes of conditioning. We have learned that certain situations require certain responses, and the very thought of not responding the way we "should" frightens us, if we even think of it at all.

When we find ourselves wearing those glasses, it is possible, through a process of acceptance and compassion, to take them off.

And even though this notion of ending the depression sounds very appealing, to a part of us it feels like death. It leaves a hole in our identity, an empty space that usually feels unbearably uncomfortable.

Making peace with emptiness,
becoming friends with spaciousness,
requires great courage.

We are sentient beings
            trying not to be sentient,
living beings tensed up against life.

That's depression.

This is what I think.
This is what I feel.
Therefore,
this is who I am,
this is reality.

When we are depressed this seems so
obviously true that questioning it never
occurs to us. And, in a narrow sense, it
is true. It's just that by believing it, we
close ourselves to universes
of
possibilities.

Thoughts and feelings are not the same.

Complete the following:
　　"How do you feel?"
　　"I'm depressed."
　　"That's not a feeling. That's a thought.
　　Look closely. How do you _feel_?"

A common pattern of confusing thoughts with feelings...

I'm depressed. Something distracts my attention from my misery. For a while I'm not aware of the depression. As soon as the distraction goes away I think,
    "Oh, I forgot. I'm depressed. I have no reason to be feeling good."

BELIEF: Depression is the only <u>appropriate</u> response to this situation in my life. <u>Anyone</u> would be depressed under these circumstances.

RESULT: The depressing thoughts re-emerge and I'm officially depressed again. "This is real. Anything else is just fooling myself."

Also, we don't need to look for excuses or justification for how we feel.

It is better to just stay focused on how we feel. Then <u>why</u> we feel that way will become apparent.

Trying to figure out
in our heads
why we are feeling a certain way just
takes us farther and farther away from
ourselves.

It is never helpful
to use a thought
to figure out
a feeling.

For example:

When grieving,

give yourself permission
to feel whatever you feel instead of having
standards about how you should be. It is
not true that certain feelings are okay and
others are not. "Okay" and "not okay" are
thoughts. When we put thoughts in charge
of feelings we get into trouble.

It's not
the feeling we're having that's a problem,
it's our judgment about that feeling.

We
could be feeling anything, and, if we
weren't telling ourselves it was wrong in
some way, there would be no problem.
The problem comes when we reject ourselves
for what we're feeling.

Our feelings are the most intimate experience we have of ourselves. Very often we think we need to blame ourselves for our feelings, or feel guilt about them, and then punish or discipline ourselves.

But really,

<u>what we do about our feelings</u> <u>determines the quality of our relationship</u> <u>with ourselves.</u>

We are responsible <u>to</u> how we feel rather than <u>for</u> how we feel.

If we can create a safe, loving place

within ourselves

for how we feel,
then we can create it
for all the aspects of who we are.

Get used to looking
to see how you feel.

Don't assume you know.

As long as we're depressed, we don't know
how we're feeling. It's only when we say
yes to ourselves and stop depressing that
how we're feeling becomes available to us.

N. - I would like to explore the relationship between the part of me who gets depressed (I call her The Saboteur) and the part of me who hates her, who is really afraid of depression. The Saboteur says, "What's the use? I might as well give up." If you're like me and have a history of depression doing you in...

Guide - But that's the whole point. It isn't the depression that "does you in." If I wake up one day very depressed and decide there's just no use in living, that's not a problem in itself. It is my reaction to the depression that can be a problem. This is true in the same way that it would be if you came to me and said, "I'm really depressed. I don't see any use in living," and I said, "You're right. Here's a gun. Shoot yourself." — Do you see? The fact that you're feeling that way isn't a problem. We can guess that if you came to me and said that, I would say something to you like, well, what's going on? how did you get to that conclusion? and you would start talking about it.

First you would talk about the "whats", the external elements of your situation. This isn't working and that isn't working and I feel this and I feel that. And then we would start talking about what's under that. Well, this is going on and that is going on. Then we'd talk about what is under <u>that.</u> Well... as we worked up through the layers, we would get to a place of, I don't like this, I don't want this, I don't want to be having this experience.

Well, you are. So, now, how can you sit still with that? How can you be with that? In our practice we take the next step of how can you embrace that? How

can you be with that as though you were
being with one of your children who came
to you and said, "Mom, I'm depressed"?
You wouldn't say, "Get out of here. I
don't want to hear that kind of talk."

The work is to develop the same relationship with yourself that you would be
willing to have with someone you love.
Actually, you would even be willing to
have it with someone you hardly know.

N.— Okay, let's talk about the one who
is really afraid of hearing that depressed
voice inside of me and wants it to go
away altogether.

Guide — Because that one is the problem.

N.— Yes.

Guide— This is where we introduce the
notion that none of this happens by

accident. Because if we simply have the one who is depressed and wants to die, that's manageable. I've been depressed and wanted to die so many times in my life that, you know, I can't take it too seriously at this point.

I say, "Oh, okay. I'm really depressed. So, now, how can I take care of myself while I'm feeling this way?"

And is it fun? No, it isn't fun. And is it going to pass? Probably. It always has before.

There are people who don't even find depression particularly troubling. They have more difficulty with things like happiness or anger. So it's just whatever a person has identified as A Really Big Problem that _is_ one for them.

So there's depression. Big Deal, right? But somebody inside me hates it and

is afraid of it. Now, if I get depressed and then get upset that I'm depressed, wouldn't you think that I would want,
          as quickly as possible,
to find out everything I could about depression so that I could manage it or master it in some way?

N. – Well, eventually, yes. I don't think, though that I'd want to do that <u>while</u> depressed ... right ?

Guide – Well, here's the part of it that's interesting to me.
          Why is it that if this is a problem and something I want to do something about,
          why is it that the thing that always arises with it is the very thing that will <u>stop</u> me from doing anything about it? The fear and hatred of it will keep me stuck, not the depression.

Let's say I have a toothache and I really hate going to the dentist, I'm afraid of going to the dentist. I put off going, and the toothache gets worse and worse. But I really don't want to go to the dentist because of my fear and hatred and the pain gets worse and worse and worse. Now, I don't know what would eventually happen. I guess the tooth would fall out or something and the pain would stop. But then what would happen? Another tooth is going to hurt, right? And there are lots of teeth!
At some point
I would have to

admit that by going to the dentist, I might not have this pain.

And so, if I remain completely invested in staying with my fear and hatred, wouldn't you become suspicious that there is another payoff for me? Such as: I get to have this miserable experience all the time.

N.— Which is what I'm familiar with.

Guide — Which is what I'm familiar with, yes.

N. — I'd rather do this than change.

Guide — Yes, so I don't think it's an accident that when this depression comes up, right along with it is the reaction that's going to maintain it.

That's one of the things we talk about here at this Center that causes many people to head for the door because it sounds so preposterous. It's just such an absurd notion.

"Why would I want to maintain depression? I hate depression. I don't want to be depressed. That's crazy; that's stupid. I'm not doing that. I want to get over this. I don't want to feel this ever again."

Well, then, stop hating it.

"How can I stop hating it? If I do that, I'll be depressed all the time. The only thing that's keeping me from being constantly depressed is that I hate depression so much."

No... do you see? The biggest difficulty, as I see it, is getting a person to be open to the possibility that what they think is going on might not be going on. Everything in our conditioning tells us that the way to get rid of something is to hate it — hate it out of existence, resist it out of existence. When we present to a person that it's the resistance that's maintaining the problem, they tend to not want to talk to us anymore.

OLD ZEN STORY*
    Bodhidharma's successor comes to
    him and cries, "My mind is not
    pacified. Master, pacify my mind."

    Bodhidharma says, "If you bring me
    that mind, I will pacify it for you."

    The successor says, "When I search
    my mind I cannot find it."

    Bodhidharma says, "Then your mind
    is pacified already."

I'm trying desperately to get rid of
something, and I can't get away from it for
a second; I drop my resistance to it,
invite it in, and it's nowhere to be found.
But when I get into a really tight spot, I'm
afraid of dropping the resistance.

* Zen Flesh, Zen Bones (1989), Anchor Books

"When you are drowning, you need to relax."

"But how can I relax when I'm drowning? That's nuts! What I have to do is fight for life!"

"No, fighting for life will kill you."

LETTING GO
- a guided imagery -

This imagery is on letting go, and it is, for me, two things. First, it is the disidentification, the movement from being identified with someone or something that is separate. Second, it is the movement back to center, to that openess, the place of acceptance, the experience of being at one with our True Nature, All That Is, Wisdom/Love/Compassion.

In this exercise, I'm going to ask you to relax and go with me as much as you can because what I'm hoping we've going to be able to do is discover, feel, and explore some of the places within us that keep us from letting go.

You can read this guided imagery, pausing at certain points to follow the instructions you are given. Another way is to make a recording and listen to it. You could record it, or you might ask a friend to do it for you.

(Begin recording here.)

Get as comfortable as you can be, the idea being to stay awake, and start with several long, deep breaths. As you take these breaths, see if you can keep your attention focused on the breath as it enters your body,
as it fills your body,
and as it leaves your body.

PAUSE   (45 seconds to 1 minute)
              longer if desired

... just being with the breath, having no concern for anything other than breathing in and breathing out...

PAUSE

Now as you allow your breath to return to normal, spend just a moment or so checking in with your body, allowing your awareness to expand to include your entire body from head to toe, being open to the body, aware of it, sensitive to it in a way that will allow it to give you any information that it has for you ...

PAUSE

Taking another long, deep breath, shift your awareness to what you are feeling, to your emotions ... once again being open, being available ...

PAUSE

... see if you can just be open to any insights your emotions might hold for you today ...... Now, another deep breath ... and allow your awareness to expand to include your mind — not trying to change

35.

anything, improve anything — just noticing.

PAUSE

And now, taking another deep breath, would you just let yourself go... just allow yourself to let go completely and absolutely... Let yourself feel what it is like when you let go completely.

PAUSE

What is this like for you? Is it like laughing, dancing, running? Perhaps as you let go, you are aware that there is something that stops you from letting go completely... So would you allow yourself to become aware of that as completely as you can for right now? What is this that keeps you from letting go? Where is it in your body? What does your body feel like when you've holding on, when you've resisting? What happens with

you emotionally when you can't let go?
What keeps you from letting go? Is it
your emotions? What is it like in your
mind when you can't let go? How does
your mind keep you from letting go?...
... And when you find something within
you that keeps you from letting go, see
if you can simply acknowledge it.
Thank it for taking care of you and
protecting you in the way that it does.

PAUSE

... And once again take a nice, deep
breath and let go... just feel yourself
let go... no restraint, no concern,
relaxing completely, absolute faith...

PAUSE

How does this feel? Is it calm? Is it
peaceful?... Letting go utterly... See if
you can take it to an even deeper level.

If you run into something that stops
you, once again see if you can just
acknowledge it, just allow it, simply
breathing in and breathing out...
nothing separating you from All That Is.

PAUSE

Just stay with these things, and when
you are ready, bring your attention
back into the room and slowly open
your eyes.

We hardly ever look at depression
because the assumption is so deep that
something is wrong with it.
Hide it.
Reject it.
Deny it.

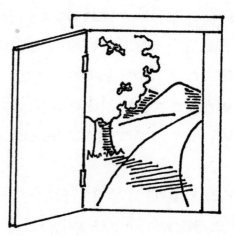

As soon as I see that it's okay, I'm free
to explore what it is.

A really good starting point is being open
to the possibility that it's nothing like
what I have thought it is.

When I was allowed to enter the monastery, my teacher began to help me with a manic-depressive tendency for which I had never sought treatment. He directed me to watch closely how I could go from being very high energy to very depressed and very depressed to very high energy. While high energy, I would have a tremendous sense of well-being, increased creativity, and a fascination with life. At other times I would feel like I could hardly get out of bed and walk across the room.

One night I was sitting in my room (in the monastery where I trained there wasn't a lot going on) focusing on the energy level in my body. I watched it get higher and higher and higher until it reached a certain point and then I watched it just plummet and collapse in on itself.

What I realized in this experience was that rather than depression being a lack of energy, which I had always thought it was — because when you can't walk across the room the logical conclusion is that you have no energy — it was actually that I had so much my body wasn't able to deal with it.

And even more than that, it wasn't so much that my body couldn't cope as that my conditioned response to myself couldn't cope. I operate within a certain range of vibration or energy or emotion, and when it gets outside of that range, it's so uncomfortable that my system overloads and circuits start to blow.

Having realized this, two things strike me as very important. First, I always encourage people to be physically active. We are animals; we are physical creatures. We are designed to move a lot and to work. Exercise helps us "use up" energy and keep our systems balanced. Someone who sits at a desk hour after hour doing stressful or boring work and who has no physical outlet for that energy can go quickly beyond the range of tolerance for their system and then go into this depression I'm describing. So I'm always encouraging people to exercise.

Second, the potential problem is that the more you exercise, the more stress you are able to cope with. People will tend  to exercise, feel better, and then take on more stress and still go to that

42.

point of failure or overload where
they become depressed.

One of the processes that we pay
close attention to in our practice goes
like this: there is movement,
sensation, a label that goes with
that, an emotional response, and
then a conditioned behavior pattern.
(see page 9) As the vibrational
level of the body gets higher
(sensation), it's sending out signals
and they are being interpreted as
anxiety or fear or pressure or stress
(labels and emotional responses), and
then the system begins to try to
cope with that (conditioned behavior
pattern).

We watch closely this process so that
we can begin to let go of the
associations we have, the labeling
system we have developed to go with

the particular sensations. We don't need to change anything. We just need to realize that sensations don't mean anything, and certainly not what we have always thought they meant.

As we understand this process more clearly, as we know that depression isn't something outside our ability to influence, we can make other choices about the level of stress that we are willing to take on, especially when we recognize that building the stress in that way, the energy level getting higher and higher in that way, is one of the first steps in depression.

EXERCISE

Write down what happens with you while
you are depressed.

- I think about this :

- I have these fantasies:

- My heart, stomach, breath do this:

- I stop eating, sleeping, exercising...:

See if you can notice how when you think
this you feel that. Notice how repetitive it is.

"How can I know these things?"   Sit quietly.
                                  Pay attention.
                                  Believe nothing.

45.

Depression

brings me back to myself
in a way much of life does not.

It gets my attention.
It brings me to a halt.

It says, "STOP! PAY ATTENTION!"
which I am usually not willing to do

for myself.

DEPRESSION: Life's way of keeping
all our emotions
from happening at once.

Depression can actually be a way of
taking care of ourselves. It can be
protection, solace, comfort. We can
view it like a soft blanket we can wrap
up in.

It's no accident that when
people get depressed they often go to
bed and eat. We attempt to return
to a sort of infant state. We reduce
the world to a simple sleep and eat
state. Get into a warm place; get
tummy full of food. We want to be
little and taken care of.

This slows us
down and gives us time to find the line
between denying ourselves and indulging
ourselves. It helps us discover what we
really need.

If you are going to be depressed,

BE DEPRESSED...

THROW YOURSELF

A DEPRESSION PARTY

SUGGESTIONS

- Bake yourself a little black cake. Don't put anything in it that would make it rise.

BLACKBERRY

BITTERSWEET CHOCOLATE

- Put on dark clothes, turn on sombre music, turn out the lights, get in bed, pull the covers over your head.

- Paint a big, dark depression picture.

What's the point, you ask?

The point is that if you do something like
this, you are letting go of your resistance
to the depression.

For instance, if you paint or draw a picture
of your depression, you have to "get
outside of it" in order to form an image
of it. In other words, you disidentify
from the parts of you who are depressed,
and from this disidentified place you are
better able to gain some perspective.
From this clearer, less painful place you
have the opportunity to embrace the
parts of you who are suffering.

A little testimonial →

One evening not long ago I was feeling really depressed. I was having the kinds of thoughts I usually have while depressed: I don't know what I want to do. I don't see any reason to keep trying. Everything is too hard. I don't like where I am but I don't want to be anywhere else, either.

Around and around these thoughts went for a while until I just suddenly said to myself,

"Okay, if I am going to be depressed, I might as well enjoy it as much as I can."

I went to the supermarket and bought several of my favorite foods...

Then I went to the video store and
rented four videos. When I got home,
I moved the television so that I could
watch a video and cook at the same
time. If I
grew tired
of one video,
I changed to
another. I
listened to
music that I
love.
I did anything that I felt like doing.

Self-indulgent? Irresponsible? Absolutely
not. The experience was one of spending
the evening with someone who loves me
unconditionally, who doesn't judge me,
who doesn't think it's wrong to pamper
myself a little when I'm feeling down.
The truth of the matter
        is that it was one of the
            best evenings I've ever had.

"How can I know when I'm being self-indulgent and when I'm truly taking care of myself?"

There is, of course, no simple answer to this question. However, here are some thoughts on the matter.

- Self-indulgence is often accompanied by a subtle or not-so-subtle undercurrent of defensiveness or belligerence.
- Taking care of oneself tends to feel like love.
- ODDLY ENOUGH, when we're being self-indulgent, it is rare that we will hear from the voice in our head that asks, "Is this self-indulgent?" It is only when we're taking care of ourselves in a loving way that the voice speaks up.

Why?

Because...

... only egocentricity is concerned with this question,

and egocentricity is the process of suffering, of inadequacy, of self-hate.

So when we are acting out of true compassion for ourselves, egocentricity fights to regain control in ways too numerous and subtle to mention.

We're doing something loving and it says, "Are you sure you're not being self-indulgent?" We're doing something self-indulgent, and it doesn't say a word.

So is egocentricity to be feared and hated? No. Fear and hate are egocentric.

Include
it in the circle of
compassionate acceptance.

Just don't believe anything it says.

"DEPRESSION" is a label.

I'm simply feeling the way I feel.

BIG QUESTION:
    How much of my problem is with the way I actually feel, and how much is with what I'm telling myself about how I feel?

One of the most commonly depressed
emotions is anger.

When we are children, anger is frightening
because it is so unacceptable to adults.
  - We feel anger, but
  - it's more threatening to have it than
    not to have it so
  - we learn to depress it because
  - we are afraid.

We often turn this anger inward against
ourselves. As adults, we can react with:

  · guilt   · illness
  · fear   · aggression
  · self-hate   · (fill in the blank)

We want to treat emotions
like house guests.

If we give them the master bedroom
with the hot tub, TV, etc., they're
never going to want to leave.

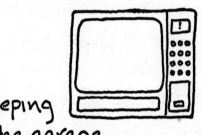

But if we throw a sleeping
bag on the floor of the garage
they won't feel welcome.

We want to find
the place in-between where they feel
welcome but know they've not invited to
stay forever.

Also,

don't meet them at the front door with a shotgun. They'll come down the chimney.

What we resist, persists.

Everyone wants what they can't have. As soon as we make something forbidden, it becomes the most desirable thing in the world. An emotion that feels rejected gets stronger. It becomes like a dog that you don't feed enough

or a child who doesn't get enough attention.

It becomes desperate.

Don't be afraid of your
feelings...

Learn to express them <u>to yourself</u>.
It is always safe to express how you
feel to yourself.

Afraid you'll lose control?

You won't. The reason we lose control is
that we haven't
expressed
our feelings.

We think we have to keep our feelings
dammed up or else there will be a flood.

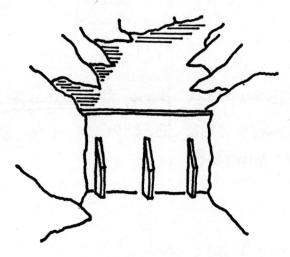

But if we never dammed them up, a flood
would be much less likely!

You can open up to yourself (dare you?)
a little at a time until the pressure is down.

All you have to do is acknowledge how you
are feeling and then treat yourself as you
would treat a friend who was feeling the
same way.

"Yes, but:
  · I should know better
  · I have no right to feel this way
  · I've done something very wrong
  · I've been treated unfairly
  · I brought this on myself
  · I da·da·ta·da·da·ta·da. "

The big question here is "So what?" The
most likely reason you're having this
experience is that you haven't loved yourself enough.
A good beating never helped anything —
        except possibly a rug —
   and aren't you tired of being one?

Taking that risk often involves learning
to trust yourself and

WE DON'T TRUST PEOPLE
WHO BEAT US UP!

If we've going to find out who we are,
we have to stop beating on ourselves
long enough to open up to ourselves
in order to find out who we are.

This is the only way
to find out
who we are.

PRACTICAL SUGGESTIONS
for changing your relationship to depression

- SET LIMITS — Say no if life is making more demands than you can meet. Instead of doing and doing until you can't take it anymore and you explode, learn to recognize the signs sooner.

- STOP BEATING YOURSELF — period.

- TAKE CARE OF YOURSELF — Do this not in a minimal, miserly sort of way because you feel that's all you deserve — but in a loving, generous way. Be kinder to yourself than you think you should be.

- DEVELOP YOUR AWARENESS — Sit quietly. Focus on your breath. Observe your thoughts and feelings, holding onto nothing, pushing nothing away. If you notice yourself tensing up, stop, and return to the breath — no judgments.

63.

SIGNS... LEADING TO EXPLOSION

✱ I shouldn't be feeling this way. ✱ I have no right to feel this way. ✱ I'm old enough to know better. ✱ I'm just being childish. ✱ It doesn't make sense for me to feel this way. ✱ It's selfish of me to feel this way. ✱ There's something wrong with me for feeling this way. ✱ I don't want to feel this way now. I don't have the strength for this today. I'll deal with this tomorrow when I'm more together. ✱ I don't have time for this today. I've got too much to do to be upset. ✱ I thought I let go of this long ago. Why is it back? What have I been doing wrong? ✱ I refuse to deal with this again. ✱ I'm too tired to do this now, but it's <u>really</u>, <u>really</u> important and I <u>absolutely</u> <u>must</u> get it done right away. ✱ I must exercise self control. ✱ I don't want to do this, but if I don't, her feelings will be hurt. ✱ I have made him dependent on me. I can't stop now. ✱ I have no choice! ✱

... and then later we ask,
"Now, how did __that__ happen?"

ACCEPTANCE

The first step is always acceptance.
Acceptance precedes even recognition.
  I will not be willing to see what I'm
experiencing until I am willing to
accept what I'm experiencing.

[Wayne Dyer has a book out titled
    I'll See It When I Believe It.]

As long as we're trying to avoid being who
we are or seeing who we are at any
level, we are doomed to remain in these
conditioned habit patterns that we suffer
over. Each time we grasp our willingness
to see these things,

                without judgment;

if possible, we take one step closer to
freedom.

66.

REMEMBER:

If you see something you don't like about the way you are and you beat yourself up for it, pretty soon you will have trained yourself to stop looking. *

Believe it or not, the only thing that gives these negative feelings any power is our fear of them. If you were to welcome them eagerly with open arms, they wouldn't appear. It's really true that the more you genuinely try to invite them, the more unavailable they are.

"All right, I'm ready...

* quoted from That Which You Are Seeking Is Causing You to Seek (1990)

... I'm going to face this. I'm willing. I'm
really going to see how this works...
   Okay, come on depression. Come on.
Where are you? Talk to me. What
have you got to say?"

BIG SILENCE

But the moment I forget and the
willingness to be open isn't there,
   and I think I've let go of depression,
   and I'm hoping I'm better,
   and I'm hoping I'll never be depressed
      again —
the moment I forget not to resist...

IT'S BACK.

Leads toward depression:
- raising your standards until you've dissatisfied
- not doing what gives your life meaning
- repressing how you are and with that depressing the life you know you could be living

Leads away from depression:
- being present
- not trying to change anything
- accepting what is

We tend to believe that if we accept things as they are without trying to change them they'll always be with us. In our experience the opposite is true. We maintain our depression by resisting it. As long as we're resisting, we've putting our energy into whatever it is we don't want.

As soon as we accept the depression, in that moment it is different.

Dear Miserable Person,
your life reflects your
attitude of mind; your
attitude of mind does not
reflect your life.
Much love,
your Heart

This is hard information to have, and we are
not suggesting that it's easy to turn
this around.

However, the fact that we believe it's hard
doesn't mean it's hard.
It just means we think it is.

We can use depression as a tool for self discovery. We can ask, "What is under this depression?"

We depress what we've experiencing for a reason. For example, I'm angry; I depress that anger, and in focusing on the depression I don't need to see that under the anger is hurt, and under the hurt is disappointment, and under the disappointment is fear.

The boss criticizes me, makes me angry. I can't express anger because I'd lose my job.
I'm disappointed because I thought the boss was a friend.
Underneath that, I'm afraid because what I thought was firm is revealed to be shaky.
I'm afraid I'm not going to make it.

Like everything in life
    depression is an ally, a gift.
It has something to teach us.

If I've never been depressed, I can't
help anyone else who is depressed.
If I've never accepted my own
depression,
                I can't be compassionate
                to anyone else's.

How do you begin to uncover what's under the depression?

You GET IT that there's a GOOD REASON* for being depressed and ACCEPT that it's OKAY to feel that way.

Start to EXPLORE what's REALLY going on.

* This GOOD REASON is almost never the one you think it is at first.

We are taught to believe that we have to
see something to believe it. As usual, the
opposite is nearer the truth.

That is: I won't SEE what's going on
with me because I BELIEVE
there's something wrong with
it ("I'm depressed, there's
something wrong with me.").

Or: I won't SEE that what's going
on with me is fear because
I BELIEVE that I'm angry and
I BELIEVE that anger is wrong.

Just for a little while
be open to the possibility that

there is nothing
wrong with you.

CENTERING
- a guided imagery -

This exercise will assist you in two primary ways. First, you will experience yourself slowing down. This makes it easier to focus your attention. Second, you will experience your "center" which is defined here as your core of wisdom, love, and compassion, your inherent goodness.

- -

(If recording, start here.)

Get as comfortable as you can, close your eyes, and take several deep breaths. Feel the air as it enters your body,
$$\text{fills your body,}$$
$$\text{and leaves your body.}$$

PAUSE

Now shift your awareness to your body... can you feel the outline of your body as it rests against whatever you are resting on?

76.

If you feel discomfort in some part of
your body, and, if you need to move to
release it, do so...

Now, shift your awareness to your feelings
... what are you feeling right now?...
calm, anxiety, anger, joy?... Where
are you feeling this feeling?... What
would be the opposite of this feeling?
Can you be aware of yourself going to
that opposite feeling in order to recognize
and know it?... Where in your body do
you feel this opposite feeling?

PAUSE

And now, shift your awareness to your
mind... How are you able to see your mind?
... who is it that is able to see your mind?
Just observe the activity that is going
on in your mind right now...

PAUSE

Now focus on the word <u>center</u> and on the concept <u>center</u> ... and now on the experience of center ...... Has your attention shifted to that place or feeling that is your center? ... If not, focus there now and just experience your center as fully as possible....... Can you become aware of the energy, the vitality, the life that is your center? ... See if you can feel that...

PAUSE

And now, let that energy begin to grow, to expand and move through your body. Feel it in your back, in your shoulders, your abdomen, your chest, upper arms, forearms and hands ... Can you feel this energy in your legs, your feet... how about in your toes? ... Can you feel it in your neck, your scalp, your face? ...... See if you can feel this energy throughout your entire body all at once.

PAUSE

Are you shifting your attention from place to place in your body to experience this feeling? ... or have you moved back from yourself in order to feel it everywhere at once? ... Look to see how you are experiencing this feeling...

PAUSE

Continue to focus on this life force, this vitality throughout your body... Where do you feel it most strongly?... Do you know how you are able to experience this feeling?... See if you can increase the feeling, intensify the sensation...

Stay with this experience for as long as you like, and when you are ready, bring your attention back into the room, and slowly open your eyes.

This moment is the only moment you have.
HAVE IT!
Don't be afraid
to experience your experience.

There is nothing to fear.
There is nothing in the universe
that wants you to suffer.

Rather than focusing on what you want
to have...or get...or do,
focus on how you are —NOW—
because how you are now
is all you'll ever experience.

Projecting into the future from a present depression causes me to see a depressing future...

I believe that what I'm experiencing is real. If I let go of that and get into the present, I realize the present is quite manageable.

> Nothing awful is going on
> except the way I feel,
> and if I didn't hate the feeling,
> it wouldn't be awful.

Coming back to the present allows me to focus on what is really going on instead of overwhelming myself with imaginings.

The feeling is only a feeling —
the label is upsetting.

How I treat myself
in depression
is more important than getting over it
or what I'll do when it's over.

Hating and rejecting myself in this moment
is not good practice
for loving and accepting myself
in another.

When I stop depressing the feelings,
I can begin to take care of the parts
of me who feel isolated,
vulnerable,
and afraid.

If I stay in the depression, I'll never see
what is underneath it.

We don't need to be afraid of our feelings
because of how we think
they're going to make
us act.

Life keeps saying...

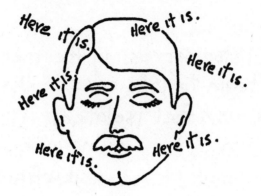

and we keep saying...

Life keeps giving us opportunities to take
responsibility and end our suffering, and we keep
turning them down!
Some practices say many are called but few are
chosen. This practice says everyone is called,
almost no one answers.

"Will you define what you mean by 'taking responsibility'?"

Guide: Yes, I am referring to starting out, right now, to respond to what is. In this evening's context, it has to do with depression and our relationship to it. However, it can be our relationship to anything.

I've chosen depression because so many people struggle with it. It tends to be something that people think is an obvious block to spiritual practice. A person who is acutely depressed will feel they have to get over the depression before they can do spiritual practice. I'm putting forth the notion that spiritual practice can be done with depression, that it is a wonderful thing to work with. So are grief and loss and illness. Anything can be a wonderful thing to work with.

If I'm committed to a spiritual practice, and one day I find myself depressed, I can begin to focus on how I do this process of depressing.

I can notice that I have always responded to depression in certain ways, and I can decide to respond to it in a different way.

What will that be like?

The way I think about this is that I am going to become the person who is going to help me with this. I'm going along in life never having felt strong or supported, and, suddenly, someone comes into my life who wants to help, who wants to give me support, who wants to listen and talk and explore things with me. On top of that, this is someone who

loves me unconditionally and is willing
to be with me <u>all the time</u>!

This person
never criticizes me or tries to change me
or thinks I should be different.

☆☆ ISN'T THAT A DREAM COME TRUE!

It would be wonderful if heaven
would open up and drop someone like
that into my life,
but have you ever
noticed how seldom
that happens?

So I realize that I can
be that person for myself.

I can come
back to a centered place,

move into
unconditional love and and acceptance
and have the same attitude toward
myself that I have

toward anyone else
I love.

We can let go
and be free
in a moment.

But will we?
Probably not.

But that just means we won't,
it doesn't mean we can't.

The difference between allowing yourself to
feel real pain or depressing that pain
                    is the difference between
            being cut by a knife
            or enveloped by fog.

The cut will heal,
usually quicker than you think,
and life can go on.

But you can live your whole life in the
fog, buffered against the experience of
pain.
                        The sadness
is that when protected from pain
we are also protected from joy.

Being depressed and unhappy sometimes
                    is just part of life.
It doesn't mean that something has gone
wrong with life any more than rain is
something that has gone wrong with the
weather

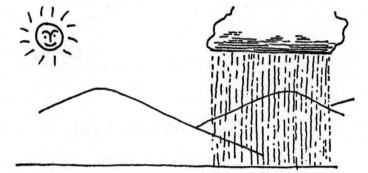

or night is something that has gone
wrong with day.

WHAT KIND OF PERSON DO I WANT TO BE ?

WHAT KIND OF RELATIONSHIP DO I WANT WITH MYSELF ?

HOW WOULD I LIKE TO TAKE CARE OF MYSELF ?

WHAT DO I DO INSTEAD ?

Put a check mark (✓) next to the things
you would say to your best friend if he/she
were depressed and came to you for help.

☐ You shouldn't be feeling that way. It's
a sign of weakness.

☐ Would a big hug from someone who
loves you help?

☐ Are you being kind and gentle with
yourself?

☐ Just stop feeling that way. It's all your
fault anyway. You asked for it.

☐ You're probably going to be depressed
forever.

☐ Can you just let yourself be depressed
without hating it?

☐ I don't want to be around you when
you're depressed.

Now, go back over the list and put a check
mark (✓) next to the things you say to
yourself when you are depressed.

Everyone has one person to take care of.

Be sure you take care of you <u>before</u> you try to take care of someone else.

AGAIN:
Learn to say YES to you <u>before</u> saying YES to others.

AND AGAIN:
Take care of your needs <u>before</u> attempting to take care of another's.

It won't make you more selfish.
It will make you more generous.

We want to try to take care of others
instead of ourselves
because
we can't take care of anyone else and
we can take care of ourselves!

What we are suggesting
is that not taking care of ourselves
is designed to perpetuate suffering.

Why would we want to perpetuate
suffering?

- It's familiar.
- It's what I think I deserve.
- It's safe.
- It's what everyone else does.
- I don't have to take responsibility.

How do you feel about having pleasure?
Explore your beliefs.

If self-denial made you a better person,
wouldn't you be one by now?

Living your life in fear
that you're going to do it wrong

is like an explorer
who is afraid of getting lost...

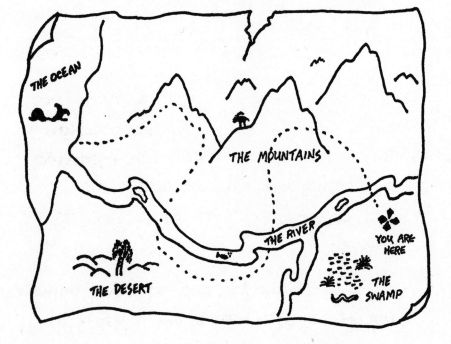

We are conditioned from childhood.
Growing up is a process of having one's
autonomy removed in order to be
socially acceptable, compliant. And
generally speaking, the better you learn
that, the worse off you are.

Finding yourself,
following your heart,
doesn't mean you're going to become
socially unacceptable.

Think about heroes, pioneers, geniuses,
inspirational people — they are focused
on that which gives their life meaning,
not on being socially acceptable.
First is commitment to being true to
themselves, second, maybe, to what
the world expects.

PROJECTION

It is good to recognize that the expecta-
tions of others, the standards they
expect us to meet, are really our own
projections. We judge ourselves by our
standards, project them out onto other
people, then believe that they think
those things about us.

A POSSIBLE SCENARIO

I'm depressed; I hate being depressed;
I'm judging myself for being depressed.
I look at my friends; I think they hate
it when I'm depressed; I think they
are judging me.

IN FACT

They may have no reaction to it at all.
They may not even notice.
It's _my_ standards that aren't being met!

YES, BUT

What if they tell me they hate my depression?

If your friends tell you they hate your depression, you can know that that's their problem just as it would be your problem if you hated theirs.

We hate and avoid in others what we've not willing to face in ourselves.

If I see a problem, it's mine. My eyes saw it; it appeared in my head; it came out of my mouth.

OH NO, SHE'S DEPRESSED AGAIN

I HATE IT WHEN I AM DEPRESSED. IT SCARES ME.

IF I REJECT HER, MAYBE SHE'LL CHEER UP.

I HATE IT WHEN YOU'RE DEPRESSED. CHEER UP.

99.

The ways I think the world expects me to be are the ways I've been taught to believe I should be.

People are judging and criticising and dismissing me all the time, but as long as I'm meeting my standards of how I should be, I don't even notice.

As soon as I don't meet my standards, I think other people know that I'm not and are judging me as harshly as I'm judging myself.

Are you willing
to give up your life
for what you think
other people
might be thinking?

Think about it.

Has giving up your own life
brought the acceptance and approval
that you've always wanted?

Has not being who you really are
brought the joy and fulfillment
you've been seeking?

We deny ourselves our life, close our options
because we think society expects us to, we
think people will judge us, we think it's too
selfish to do otherwise.
We take the path
that seems safest.

Then, because we're depressing our
passion, our desire for life, we eventually
move into despair and ask ourselves,
Why go on?

A valid question.

We end up with just the hard stuff,
the shoulds,
the have tos,
the things we were trying to avoid in
the first place

We wind up with emptiness
exhaustion
meaninglessness.

The good news is
    none of what society or culture
    tried to get you to believe was
    true in the first place.

There never have been any limits.
There never was anything wrong with you

                  and there still isn't.

You can be whatever you choose,
and the proof of that is that
you are now.

When I'm feeling good,
        I'm a good person.
When I'm feeling bad,
        I'm a bad person.

If I'm happy, I'm right, I'm good.
If I'm not, I'm wrong, I'm bad.

The choice of words in our language shows
the priority "happy" has.

    Depression can happen
when we try not to be unhappy.

We want to go from one peak to the next

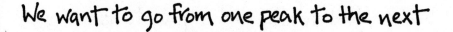

without traveling through the valleys below.

peaks/valleys   up/down   right/wrong
  -one cannot exist without the other-

If what we think is wrong with us
were really wrong with us,
we would have been able to fix it by now...

The fact that we haven't been able to fix
it is the proof that it's not really the
problem.
      The problem is that we have
been taught to believe there's a problem.
It's like being told that something is
broken and trying and trying to fix it and
never succeeding.
      Because it isn't broken.

There is no problem.
Stop creating one.

Feeling guilty over being
how you are
                    does nothing
but rob you of your life.

It is okay to
    feel whatever you feel
    think whatever you think
    be however you are.

Guilt and fear keep us from knowing our
True Self, our intrinsic purity and
goodness, the Divine within us.

    Whatever you are doing, love your-
    self for doing it. Whatever you are
    thinking, love yourself for thinking
    it.

If you don't like it, love yourself for not
                            liking it.

107.

Can you be open to the possibility that
if you were who you really are you
would have the approval and acceptance
you've always wanted? — From yourself
if from no one else?

The only approval we really care about
is our own.
            If I feel I've done a good job,
I feel good. If not, I don't.
                        It doesn't
actually matter to us what others think.

PROJECTION, AGAIN

Here's how it works in part:

LOOP: I won't be who I am because I'm afraid others won't approve → I try to be who I "should" be and I don't approve → I don't approve of me → I project that disapproval onto others and then believe they disapprove of me → I feel disapproved of → Therefore, it seems that I have proof that there's something wrong with me.

And there kind of is.

I'm caught in this awful loop
of my own making.

IRONY:

We endlessly seek other people's approval

      when the only approval
      that means anything to us

                is our own.

If I'm living the life
            I want to live
it's clear
that nobody owes me anything,
and from that place of
being satisfied

I can be much more generous.

III.

Whatever you do, recognize that you are doing it for you and enjoy it.

If you realize you no longer want to do it,
STOP.

"Isn't that irresponsible?"
You'll never know until you stop and find out. You could practice with some of the many little things you do and hate but continue to do because you believe you should or someone told you you should.

If you're responsible
because you're afraid not to be,
you're not responsible,
you're afraid.

People know things they stopped doing when they started growing up. Here are some we came up with. Can you add your own?

playing in the woods
lying on back, watching clouds
knowing god
skating
playing baseball
drawing and painting
singing
getting excited about holidays
reading a book over and over
scribbling
playing in puddles

We have to face eventually that we
don't want to be undepressed.
Terrible things might happen to us if
we're not depressed!

We have our
identity in this process of depressing.
We are afraid that if we stop, we
won't know how to be,
won't know who to be,
won't know what life will expect.

It is safer and more comfortable to
continue with the depressing than to
risk the freedom.

Is this depressing?

Can I realize I do this (reject well-being)
without being depressed about it?

It's depressing
to realize that I've spent my whole life
depressing myself.

The most depressing part is that I've
thought it was external. Now I'm getting
the sense that it is something I've
learned to do and now do to myself.

To say this is
depressing information is like saying
that you are on a sinking ship and
you have just discovered a lifeboat...

You can stand there and be upset that the ship is sinking, or you can take the lifeboat.

The lifeboat is the information in this book.

Take it and go.

Don't waste any time.

The perspective of this book is that there is nothing more important than compassion.

The compassion we've talking about might not look nice and polite. It doesn't necessarily mean doing what others want you to do or being how they want you to be.

We've talking about being compassionate with yourself because everything else springs from that.

IT IS NOT SELFISH
TO LOVE YOURSELF.

If you can't find compassion for yourself, you'll never find it for anyone else. You won't know how.

You will never be truly generous to anyone else while depriving yourself.

The reason we don't tell
anyone they <u>should</u> do
this is that a person
<u>won't</u> do this until
                they've ready.

Most people never will, in this life.

All we've saying is that
                    when you're ready
            here's the way you can do it.

This is definitely not another stick with
which to beat yourself!

        When you've suffered enough,
you'll remember that you know how to do it.

It doesn't really matter what you have thought, believed, felt or done before.

This is a new day.

"But I've always done it this way."
"But I've always been this way."
"This is just how I am."

These are three of the world's WORST EXCUSES.

It is okay to change.
It is okay to try something new.
It is okay to try something rather
radically new such as the approach we
are offering in this book. (There isn't
really anything new about it. It's just new
to many people in our culture.)

Because if you try it and don't like it, you
can always return to how you were doing
it before. No problem. No shoulds. Trying
something once or twice doesn't mean
you ever have to do it again if you don't
want to.

And not taking a risk because you are
afraid is a grave disservice to yourself.
Fear is not the problem. You can have
your fear and allow it to stop you, or you
can have your fear and risk anyway.
Either way, the fear is there. The choice
is yours.

Meditation has been practiced throughout
the world for thousands of years. In
cultures where meditation has been an
integral aspect of religious life,
practitioners have learned that sitting in
a certain posture — spine straight, body
relaxed — is most conducive to being able
to stay present. Physical pain and
sleepiness are both minimized by sitting
in this position.

A MEDITATION POSTURE

Sit on the first ⅓ of the cushion. If you are sitting on a bench, sit well forward.

Adjust your leg position until you find one that can be maintained comfortably.

Straighten your posture by pushing up from the base of the spine. Imagine that you are trying to touch the ceiling with the crown of your head. The chin will tuck slightly as you do this.

The pelvis tilts slightly forward.

The shoulders and abdomen relax.

The eyes are open, slightly out of focus, and lowered, looking at the floor or wall at a 45° angle.

The hands are in the cosmic mudra. The right hand is positioned a few inches below the navel, palm up. The left hand, also palm up, fits inside the right hand. The tips of the thumbs touch lightly, forming an oval.